AS LONG AS I HAVE BREATH

AS LONG AS I HAVE BREATH

Moments for Prayers
and Prayers for the Moment

REV. ALFRED R. TWYMAN, JR.

Epigraph Books
Rhinebeck, New York

Biblical verses are quoted from the following versions of the Holy Bible:
King James Version (KJV)
New King James Version (NKJV)
Revised Standard Version (RSV)
New Revised Standard Version (NRSV)
New Living Translation (NLT)

Paperback ISBN 978-1-954744-38-7
eBook ISBN 978-1-954744-39-4

Library of Congress Control Number 2021917787

Book design by Colin Rolfe

Epigraph Books
22 East Market Street, Suite 304
Rhinebeck, NY 12572
(845) 876-4861
epigraphps.com

This book is dedicated to Mary Elizabeth Johnson,
who gave me life and led me to God,
and
Sondi Elizabeth Johnson, who blessed my life and is a
daily reminder of God's unending grace.

Amen

I love the Lord because he hears
and answers my prayers.
Because he bends down and listens,
I will pray as long as I have breath!
—Psalms 116:1–2 (NLT)

CONTENTS

PREFACE:
Why I Write Prayers

The most humbling experience!

A relationship with God is the most humbling experience one can ever encounter. It calls into question our ability to put all the cumbersome luggage of this fleshly existence aside and pack lightly for a journey that is built on a promise. Sometimes we find ourselves riddled with uncertainty, fear, dread, and anger because we cannot touch this mystery. We can only have hope and faith that God's promises are true. We want constantly to fall back to the world in scripted belief that it is solid ground when, as the old hymn states, "It is sinking sand." So, we must steadfastly walk in a direction of faith toward the heart of a God who imagined us into a life that is but a breath. That is the humbling experience of a life lived with God.

Prayer has much to do with humility, that ability to acquiesce to something greater than ourselves. Prayer is directed to a personal God who loves us and hears us; it is a cry from heart to heart, from spirit to spirit.[1] There is nothing greater than God. "For this reason,

---

[1] Henri J. Nouwen, *The Road to Peace*, (Maryknoll, NY: Orbis Books, 1998), 210.

we must bow our knees to the Father of our Lord Jesus Christ" (Ephesians, 3:14, KJV).

Many of the prayers in this book were originally created for and given to incarcerated individuals who were being received into the New York State prison system. They were written and handed out so that people could not only have a moment of prayer—but also have a prayer for their moments. The theme for the prison where I worked was "where the process begins." While the prison was preparing inmates for their time of incarceration, I wanted to prepare them for their continued journey with God, regardless of their surroundings. Incarcerated people often feel that they have been taken from the world. When they come to prison, prayer offers them freedom and a place in the world. "Prayer is not an escape from the world but an entrance into it. We become conscious in prayer of how much the world is with us and how much we are in the world."[2]

"For someone who is in prison, true hope lies not simply in an early release date, but in the knowledge that in God's world there are no walls. The only walls that can hold them back are the walls that divide their hearts. Even within prison walls a heavenly garden can be cultivated by fostering a beloved community."[3] That heavenly garden can be grown out of the rich soil of prayer.

---

[2] Ann and Barry Ulanov, *Primary Speech: A psychology of prayer,* (Atlanta, John Knox Press, 1982), 4.

[3] Marianne Williamson, *Everyday Grace: Having Hope, Finding Forgiveness, and Making Miracles,* 2nd ed. (New York: Riverhead Books/Berkley Publishing Group/Penguin Group-USA, 2004), 177.

Prayer should be a natural event. To pray is to live and to live is to pray. Prayer is the avenue to our world in its truest form. In true prayer we yield to the will of God. It is the acknowledgment that we live in God's Kingdom and that the core of our very existence, our needs and our wholeness in this life and the next, lay with God. Prayer is the bridge that takes us out of the façade of earthly desires and into the reality of an all-present God. It means entering into communion with the One who loved us before we could love.[4] In a breath, in the blink of an eye, we can stop to remove the chains of our fleshly bondage and find freedom in a God whose Son says "come to Me all of you who labor and are heavy laden and I will give you rest." We can breathe. We can pray. We can have a relationship with God. We can draw near to God and God to us. We can find the life in our dying in the world and living for God.

No matter how hard goes the battle of life,
God's children need never despair.
His conquering grace giveth peace 'mid the strife.
There is wonderful power in prayer.[5]
—Rev. Alfred R. Twyman, Jr.

---

[4] Nouwen, *The Road to Peace*, 17.
[5] Eliza E. Hewitt and Fred A. Fillmore, lyricist and composer, "Wonderful Power in Prayer," *Hymnal of the Church of God*, (Anderson, IN: Warner Press, 1953), 407.

PRAYERS FOR
GREETING A
GLORIOUS
MORNING

THANK YOU, GOD!

God,
For getting me up this morning
and putting me in a right mind
that is seeking to be the mind of Christ ...
thank You!

God,
For breathing the breath of life
into my body and
allowing this vessel of flesh yet another day
to live and do Your will ...
thank You!

God,
For allowing me yet another chance
to offer and seek forgiveness
and face a sinful world with a heart
ready to deal with the sin that dwells in me ...
thank You!

God,
For offering me salvation through
a love so great that You gave us
Your son in order that we may have

eternal life.
And should I continue to believe in Him,
even in death,
I may come to live in Your heavenly kingdom ...
thank You!

God,
I am grateful for all
that You are;
and all that You have given me.
Your mercy is unending,
Your compassion infinite,
and Your love constant.
So, each evening before I close my eyes
and each morning when I rise, I will ...
thank You!
Amen.

A DAILY PRAYER

Today I am going to listen and open my heart
to the living Word that dwells amongst us.
I will heed that Word in such a way that I do not
stray from the path of righteousness.

Today I will live,
not just in accordance with the laws
of humankind, but in accordance with Your laws.
I will seek to do Your will and not mine.
Today I am going to stay in prayer to You.
I will pray for Your guidance and presence in all mat-
ters.
I will not hold sacred the devices of this world
that seek to replace You with
an other-than heavenly promise.
No, I will seek You with all my heart,
body, mind, and soul.

Today, I am going to love others
regardless of how I am treated.
I am going to bless all those I know and do not know.
I am not going to defile myself or others by
engaging in slanderous conversations,
anger, hatred, or hostility that would

cause me to sin against You.
Should I speak, it will be with words that
speak respectfully of others and praise for You.

Today I will forgive.
I will seek to have unyielding patience and
compassion for those who have trespassed against me.
I will seek forgiveness of my sins from You
and from those I have trespassed against;
for I know Your mercy is everlasting.

Today I intend to live as Your humble servant,
standing on Your promises.
I do not know that I will be here tomorrow;
for it is not promised.
But I do know that nothing in this life
will have meaning or truth unless I recognize that
everything begins and ends with You—today.

Amen.

TODAY

Today ...
Listen more than you talk.
Pray with each breath.
Seek light in the darkness.
Love all, even those who revile you.
And remember, God is always in our midst.

Amen

SIMPLE PRAYERS OF THE DAY

MORNING

God, be with me today.
Keep me humble in spirit.
Let me be guided by love.
Fill me with kindness.
Set peace in my heart.
Surround me with the Holy Spirit.
Cover me in the blood of Christ.
Let Your Word give me strength.
And keep Your praises on my lips.
Amen.

NIGHT

God, I thank You for the gift of another day.
Please stay with me in the night.
Help me to see Your light as I lay in darkness.
Lift the fear from my heart and fill it with wisdom,
that I may wake in the day patient and filled with
love.
Take the anger of all perceived wrongs from me
and let me rise in the morning with a will to forgive.
Abide with those whom I love
and sustain them in Your saving grace.
Purify my soul

and let it be touched by the Holy Spirit.
Transform my pain and suffering
to hope and faith through Jesus Christ.
And set in me a clean spirit,
that I may see a new dawn with the desire to serve
You.
Amen.

God's mercy is there for all to see.
But first we must go down on bended knee.
Pray early and often.

PRAYERS FOR
THOSE WE
LOVE

A PRAYER FOR MOTHERS

God, please bless the mothers!
They are the bearers of hope and the keepers of our
dreams.

Bless them for carrying the life that You knew existed
before they bore us.
Bless them for the faith in You that they have
imparted in us.
Bless them for their unflinching courage and strength
in times of struggle.
Bless them for their compassion when all others fail
to care.
Bless them for the comfort they bring in the midst of
our pain.
Bless them for the joy they bring to our lives that
serves to enrich our souls.
Bless them for being Your angels, Your apostles, and
Your disciples who are sometimes wrapped in the
same body of unbelievable spiritual strength and
love.

God,
Bless these women who stand with, behind, and in
front of Your children, and stay with us from birth
to death.

Bless them for their unconditional love that reminds
us of Your unconditional love. For it was a mother
that bore the greatest sign of Your love for all of
us, a Son who died on the cross for our sins. God,
please bless the mothers! Amen.

BLESS OUR CHILDREN

Behold, children are a heritage from the Lord.
The fruit of the womb is a reward.
—Psalms 127:3 (NKJV)

God, please bless our children.

Fill them with joy. Not just the joy of play and friendship, but the indescribable joy of having their hearts filled with grace and love for You. Protect and gather them as a hen gathers her brood under her wings. Incubate in them the desire to praise You. Do not allow them to be mired in the fears of the world of flesh, but set their souls in the fear of You that is the beginning of wisdom. Set Your face to shine upon them so they can come to know that, with You, their souls cannot be rendered in darkness. Please hear their prayers. Allow them to sing and make melodies that the whole of heaven may know of the songs that come not from their lips but from their souls as they stand as a chorus of voices giving thanks to You at all times for everything in the name of Jesus Christ.

Amen.

A PRAYER OF SEPARATION FROM FAMILY

God,

I am away from those I love. I cannot communicate with them as I would like. The circumstances of my life have strained our relationship and created friction and pain. We are separated by space that only you can overcome. I ask that You bless them and keep them. Make them safe in time of trouble. Do not allow them to fall into temptation or suffer unduly. Please keep love in their hearts and let not our separation bring them unbearable sorrow.

God, anoint the children in my life. Give them the knowledge to stay on Your path and not be guided by those who have strayed from you. Do not let them be vulnerable to any influence except Yours. Keep them humble and let the Holy Spirit knit their hearts in time of distress.

God, please continue to bless the older members of my family. Keep them in their right mind and spirit, that they may continue to praise You at all times. Give them the gifts of good health in their bodies and the wealth of Your abiding grace. Allow them unending growth in wisdom so that they will help us all stay rooted in You.

God, please look upon me as a sinner who wants to strengthen my relationship with You and with those whom I love with all my heart. Make the bond stronger each day I live. In Your hands I commit us all, because I do not know when I will see them again, but I know You see us all—all the time. I humbly remain Your loving servant who seeks to dwell eternally in the Holy Spirit and be bathed in the blood of Jesus Christ who draws us near the cross.

Amen.

Our relationship with God is not about power and status. It is about service, humility, and love.

PRAYERS FOR
FAITH IN
GOD

O MY LORD

O my Lord,
make it clear to me
that toward You there is fear in me.
Let my soul draw near to Thee
with a hope so clear to me
that my faith is constantly here with me.

Amen.

A PRAYER OF EMPTYING OUT

God, please take this
pain from my heart
and fill it with love!
If my body is in pain,
that, I can stand.
But to know the pain
of a heart longing for the flesh of the world
is unbearable.
So, God, take the emptiness
that has caused me pain
and fill it with the emptiness
that is the longing for You.

Amen.

A SHORT PRAYER OF PRAISE

Praise be to God!

From the moment I wake until I close my eyes, I will praise the Lord, my God. He is worthy to be praised above all else. In Him lay the hope of all eternity and infinite forgiveness. So, I will praise Him and raise my voice to speak His name in every waking moment. He is the song that plays in my mind. Every note fills me with His love.

He gave me life and holds me in the safety of His grip. He binds up my enemies and sets me on the path of Truth. I will fear Him and walk the path to Wisdom. I will worship Him and find the path to peace. I will bow down on my knees and lift my hands to acknowledge His glory. I want only to draw close to Him and seek Him with all that is within me. He is the answer to my every prayer.

He set a Messiah amongst us who died on the cross for our sins. He set the Holy Ghost in our midst to comfort us. He listens to the sins confessed in our hearts and hears our every voice. There is nothing on the earth, under the earth, or in the heavens more worthy to be praised.

Praise be to God!

Amen.

*No one is lost if their compass is faith and
their navigational aids are love, humility, and
forgiveness—and their destination is
the heart of God.*

PRAYERS FOR
SUMMONING
HOPE

OUT OF THE DARKNESS

In my darkness, O God
of light.
I live in the hope
that You make day from night.

In my fear, O God
of hope,
I ask that You set me
in a place to cope.

It is through my faith in You
that I thrive.

Because dying in the Spirit of your Son
keeps me alive.

GOD, HELP ME WITH
THE STRUGGLE

Dear God,

Please help me with the struggle of this life. Let me not give in to the temptation to quit and find myself lost in the midst of everyday sorrows. Help me look to You for hope. You are the hope that manifests itself through the death and resurrection of your Son, Jesus Christ. That He could march resolutely to the cross for our salvation has given way to the hope for the forgiveness of our sins and the other-worldly promise of everlasting life. In the midst of the struggles of this life I remember Your Son and Your promise, and I am heartened by the love You have imparted to us through Jesus Christ. And I realize that any struggle can be overcome.

Amen.

A PRAYER OF HOPE

The Lord is my portion, saith my soul;
therefore will I hope in him.
—Lamentations 3:24 (KJV)

God,
You are my hope in the midst of all my troubles;
the oasis in my desert of struggle.
When I am alone in the dark of the night,
You are the unflickering candle in the darkness.
When I am lost in the confusion of human events,
I know that You will be my guide.
When others turn from me,
I know I can always turn to You.
When my faith in others is lost,
my faith in You will never be in vain.
In my constant wanderings down the path of pain,
You are the Balm in the Gilead.
When I lament upon my brokenness,
I come to understand my wholeness with You.
And when I find the emptiness of the flesh
    unbearable,
You bring me to the fullness of a spirit longing for you.

Amen.

There are moments in my life when fear grips my soul. Yet, in the midst of my trials, I turn to the light of God to illuminate the darkness of fear.
That's hope.

PRAYERS FOR
RELEASE &
DELIVERANCE

GOD, TAKE THIS ANGER
FROM MY HEART

God,
Please take this anger from my heart!
It is an anchor on my soul that only
serves to drag me into the depths of Hell.

Help me to go from revenge to reverence.
I want to honor and respect others rather than curse
them.
Let me not be a fool who gives into anger
and seeks misplaced justice by repaying evil for evil.
But make me a prudent person who ignores insults
by humbly turning the other cheek.

Help me to go from loathing to loving.
I want to learn to love my enemies
and pray for those who persecute me.
First, open my heart that I may come to love myself.
I must seek always to love the person in the mirror,
and not the darkness of the shadow of vanity,
that I may love my neighbor as myself.

Help me to go from violence to peace.
I do not want to be overcome by evil
but want to overcome evil with good.

Teach me to live peaceably with all.
Instill Your peace in my heart!
For it is through that peace that I can maintain my
spirit
and live in unity with others.

Amen.

BRING ME TO MY KNEES
IN PRAYER

Lord,
Teach me to pray and not give up.
Keep me on the bended knee of my heart,
constantly seeking You.

In the good times when the abundance of life
is at my fingertips and I have plenty;
do not let me become arrogant
or lack charity and compassion for others.
Bring me to my knees in prayer.

When I am faced with anger
that can poison my soul,
and destroy all who love me,
only You can keep my soul intact.
Bring me to my knees in prayer.

When I am suffering
from illness and my body betrays me,
I know that You are the source of my healing.
Bring me to my knees in prayer.

When those who love me are struggling,
and I cannot be there to give them what they need,

I know that You are the source of their relief.
Bring me to my knees in prayer.

When my spirit is being attacked by the Evil One,
and I am engulfed in fear
when the darkness of this world
seeks to blot out my very soul,
I know You are the source of all hope.
Bring me to my knees in prayer.

Lord,
You are the source of my salvation.
In all things I give You glory.
Mold me to become a living prayer.
And in this life and the next,
bring me to my knees in prayer.

Amen.

A SHORT PRAYER
AGAINST REVENGE

Dear God,

In a world where revenge born out of anger and ignorance is masquerading as honor, and an "eye for an eye" has become justification for senseless violence, please guide my soul to the infinite possibilities that You present to me when my heart is filled with love. God, help me to love the righteous and the unrighteous. Restrain my anger and my desire for revenge when I feel that I have been wronged. Keep me away from the spiritual blindness that will result in taking an eye for an eye. Let me never forget that vengeance is Yours and that You will vindicate Your people and have compassion on Your obedient servants. When I am faced with fight or flight, let my response be with love.

Amen.

GOD, DELIVER ME FROM EVIL

Dear God,

Take me out of the darkness and put me into the light. Heal me of the doubt and fear that seeks to pull me into the very depths of Hell. Pull me from the grip of cruelty. Help me to understand that You are not a God of revenge and violence but one of love. When I am full of jealousy, envy, and anger, turn me back to the fruits of love, patience, and humility. When my heart is hardened with conceit and vanity, turn me back to gentleness and kindness. Set my soul on fire with the desire to speak and live Your word. Help me to see through the veil of deceit that threatens to separate me from You. When all around me the workings of the flesh attempt to set my soul in sin, deliver me from evil and make me an instrument of Your peace. To You be all honor and glory.

Amen.

A PRAYER OF HUMILITY TO SUBMIT TO GOD'S WILL

Dear God,

I delight to do Your will. I have done the things the world demands of me, and I can find no peace. Each day is trying. I am under attack from forces I cannot fight alone. I struggle on a path that leads me nowhere. I have come to a point in my life where I am afraid to close my eyes at night. I wake in the morning with fear in my heart, unable to see clearly to the end of the day. I need Your help to survive. Please do not take Your mercy away from me.

I must not lean on my own understanding but yield to You and be delivered. You are my King and the Source of all my strength. No human being can give me what You offer me. Only You can make me whole by filling me with the love that comes from my acceptance of the Holy Spirit as my comforter.

All my desires are known to You. I cannot hide my innermost feelings nor can my heart hold the truth from You. I ask that You look into my heart and see the pain and fear of one who has embraced the things of this world rather than looking to You with my whole heart. Look into my heart and see a child who longs for the embrace that only You, my Holy Parent, can give. Help me deal with the desires of the flesh—and forgive my sins. Strengthen me according to Your Word. Humble me, O Holy One! Bring me to my knees so that I may be a living prayer. I am Your humble and loving servant. I willingly submit to You, for You are the Lamp to my feet and the Eternal Light to my path.

Amen.

A PRAYER OF FREEDOM

God,
When I allow myself to be imprisoned by those
who can kill my body but cannot kill my soul,
I know that I need not be afraid of them.
For my bondage does not come from
the shackles that can be set by those of this world;
only those I put on myself.
My freedom and my bondage are with You who can
destroy both
soul and body.
I yield to You.
You offer me freedom.

God,
Often, fear guides my every move,
and I am constantly pulled in every direction,
only to find myself gripped by unyielding anger
that leaves me lost in a forest of destructive emotions.
You are the source of the map that guides me back to
the path.
You offer me freedom.

God,
Sometimes I feel like I am falling into the seemingly
unending dark pit

of shame and guilt,
unable to forgive and ask for forgiveness.
I am paralyzed by pride and fueled by a vengeful
heart
that puts me into the throes of despair
and makes me unable to seek redemption.
Yet, Yours is the hand that pulls me from the abyss.
You offer me freedom.

God,
When I am earthbound by the weight of my sin,
You lift me from those binds.
Yours are the only binds that tie.
In You I find my salvation.
You alone allow me to take flight in the freedom of
redemption,
able to soar in the shadow of Your wings.
My soul draws near to You and my heart is filled with
a love that breaks the shackles of spiritual slavery.
And I know that, despite all the troubles of this world,
Yours is the otherworldly promise of eternal life;
in that promise I know I am ready to live rightly in
this life.
Thank You for offering me freedom.

Amen.

PRAYER OF PRAISE

Dear God,
I praise You.

When I am riddled with fear and my troubles hem
me in,
I praise You.

When all who have promised their love turn from
me in my hour of need,
I praise You.

When I cannot focus, and memories of iniquities
riddle my mind and trouble my heart,
I praise You.

When the material things of this world are no longer
in my grasp,
I praise You.

When hypocrites say I am unworthy of Your love,
You continue to answer my prayers, and ...
I praise You.

In my moments of loneliness, when the pain of my

solitude racks my body, and in the darkness of my
room in the middle of the night, where no human
being can shed a light, I know You are the candle that
helps me rail against the darkness and ...
I praise You.

When my body betrays me and my health fails,
I know You offer me healing and a return to
wholeness, and ...
I praise You.

But, should this earthly vessel fail, I know that You
will bring me into the depths of Your heart in the
next life, where my soul may continue to live as a
vessel of praise, and ...
I praise You.

God, I will praise You at all times—in the morning,
noon, and night; in song, thought, and deed; in good
times and bad; in bondage and freedom.

You have redeemed me and taken me from the lowest
depths of human suffering to the highest heights of
enduring love. For You alone are God from whom all
blessings flow, and who is always worthy to be praised.
And I will keep Your praises in my heart, that they
may continually be on my lips.

Amen.

A PRAYER FOR A NEW SPIRIT

God,
Do not take Your Holy Spirit from me!
Cast the Holy Spirit in me so that I may know
Your presence and be delivered from evil.
God,
Let the Holy Spirit teach me to walk toward the
cross!
I want to humbly bear the crown of thorns in this life
in order to wear the crown of victory in the next.
God,
Let the Holy Spirit bond me to others in love,
rather than a divisive spirit that cuts with anger.
Create in me a clean heart.
Rid me of the contempt I have for others,
that the power of the Holy Spirit may stifle my un-
clean thoughts and deceitful tongue.
God,
Renew the Spirit in me each day
so that I may maintain a humble heart
and never cease to utter Your praise,
each moment that I live.

Amen.

*Prayer is music for the soul. But music would be
hard to understand if there were no silence.
To compose music is to write notes but also to put
what we call rests or moments of pause and silence
between the notes. Just as these rests between the
notes in music enhance a musical composition,
it is the silence in prayer that enhances
our experiences with God.*

PRAYERS FOR
HEALING

HEAL US

Dear God,

   From the depths of our despair, we ask that You heal the land and cast out this virus from among us. Make it so that we can be gathered together as Your people in the circle of life. Please take the fear and anxiety from our hearts and instill us with boundless faith, enduring love, and hope with no limits. Heal the sick, strengthen the fearful, and impart wisdom upon those who lead in these trying times. We ask all this in the name of Your Son, Jesus Christ, who through His sacrifice reminds us of Your unending glory. We are Yours in Him.

Amen.

A CRY FOR HELP IN THE
MIDST OF SUFFERING

O God,

Please do not turn Your face from us! Please help us in our time of suffering. Our sorrow is so deep, and the pain of our suffering racks our souls. We cry out to You because it is more than we can stand. We cannot understand why this struggle is so difficult. Did You bring this upon us? Are You even there? In our hour of need please be with us!

Help us to understand that, while weeping may remain for the night, joy comes in the morning. Guide us … dear God … guide us to the morning of our lives. Help us to trust in You with all our hearts and to lean not to our own understanding. Each day we face the possibility to be in the midst of suffering. But God, in this seemingly chaotic world, You have embedded in us the wisdom that You are *The Constant* that keeps us afloat lest we are drowned in our sorrows.

God … heal the open wounds of our hearts and help us to understand that the scars of our suffering are there to remind us that, regardless of what we have endured, *You* are the balm that makes our hearts whole. Help us to grieve our losses and do not let them embitter us; draw us closer as faithful servants who are full of compassion and love desiring to do *Your* will in *Your Kingdom.*

Let us be bathed in Your grace, O Lord, that we may soak our sorrows in the healing pool of Your promise of eternal life. It is through You that we find the strength to face our struggles, because it is through You that we can lay claim to all *hope.* We will continue to utter Your praises our whole life long—because You are the Amen to our Hallelujah.

Amen ... Amen ... Amen.

A LAMENT OF RESTORATION

God,
I cry out to You when all have left me!
Please hear my plea.
I am crippled by extraordinary illness.
The evil that exists in my body is legion.
I am exiled and chained, and I live in the tombs of
society.
Hopelessness and isolation have become my plight.
I am in bondage to the Evil One.
The rattle of my chains is a warning to
all who approach.
Those whom I love have turned from me,
and others show me no mercy.

But this I call to mind:
You are a God of endless mercy.
Your love and forgiveness have no limits.
I know that You will break the chains of
my bondage and set my soul free.
You will never forsake me.
Through You I will be restored to those whom I love,
and my tears of sorrow will turn into those of joy!

So, into Your hands I commit my spirit,
that I may be reconciled with the Holy Spirit

and healed and redeemed through He who died on
the cross.

Amen ... Amen ... Amen.

GUIDE US, DEAR GOD

Guide us, dear God, guide us in this time when our dear sister is in the midst of pain and is struggling for her life. Keep her in Your hands and help us trust in You with all our hearts and lean not to our own understanding. We ask that You be with her and ease her pain in the midst of her suffering.

Continually remind us in our hearts that You, O God, are The Constant that keeps us afloat, lest we are drowned in our fears and sorrows. Give us strength and help us understand that in our suffering and the suffering of others, You are always there. Help us grieve and do not allow us to be bitter, or angry, or even confused. Draw us closer to You as faithful servants who are full of compassion and love, desiring to do Your will in Your Kingdom.

Let us never forget that we, like our dear sister, are pilgrims who are on a journey to Your heart. And it is through You that we find the strength to face the dusk of our lives. Because it is through You that we can lay claim to all hope.

Amen.

*Dear God—is Your silence one of suffering with us?
Or is it one of peace, that through the breath of the
Holy Spirit we are to find strength in Your silence?*

PRAYERS FOR
SACRED &
STATELY
OCCASIONS

A COMMUNION PRAYER

God,

You are my rock and the foundation of my life. I draw all my strength from You. On this day of the Lord's Supper, I want to rest securely in the body of Your Son, Jesus Christ. I want to be united with my brothers and sisters in Christ through the Holy Spirit and live a life constantly speaking Your Word through faith.

God, as I draw the cup of salvation to my lips, let me never forget that You have known me from my mother's womb. You gave me life and breathed the Holy Spirit into me. All that I am or ever will be I owe to You.

As I partake of the new covenant through your Son, I want to die of my old self that I may live in the newness of life with You. And when I pass from this life, please draw me near through the Holy Spirit.

God, please do not stop working in my life, because without You I am lost. Forgive my sins and help me forgive myself. Make me a vessel of love and compassion living in this world as I prepare for the next. Break the yokes of my bondage to envy, anger, and greed. Stop my covetous behavior.

God, please bless my family, keep me in prayer, and

set my mind and heart only to that which pertains to You.

Amen.

A PRAYER FOR PENTECOST

Come Holy Spirit!
Bring me to repent,
that I may enter God's Kingdom.

Teach me to forgive,
that I may be forgiven.

Cast in me perfect love,
that the fear of this world will be cast out of me.

Give me wisdom,
that I may fear God, who can take both body and soul.

Make me lean not on my own understanding,
but seek God's path.

Humble me and remove all pride,
that I may receive God's grace.

Give me the gift of knowledge,
that I may contribute to the world and not take from it.

Impart in me the desire to always speak and live
God's Word,
that I may live in Truth.

Strengthen me for my spiritual journey,
that I remain focused on God's promises.

Make me compassionate,
in order to do unto others as I would unto myself.

Bring me to unity with others,
that I may always live in the Body of Christ.

Mold me in the Image of Christ,
that I may carry the cross each day of my life.

And draw me close to God in this life,
that I may come to dwell in God's heart in the next.

Amen.

ADVENT PRAYER
OF COMMITMENT

God,

Into Your hands I commit my spirit.

Let me never forget that Christ destined me in his love, and that I have redemption through the cross. Instill in me the desire to keep a right relationship with others. Should I become angry, deter me from sin. When I am trespassed against, open my heart to unending forgiveness. When faced with pride, humble me to become like a child so that I may enter the Kingdom of Heaven. Lead me in Truth so that I may remain an honest witness to our salvation through Jesus Christ.

May my faith be deeply rooted, that I may always return upright to You despite the winds of sin and the storm of evil that surround me. Keep me in prayer so that I am always seeking You. Incline my heart to love You first and allow my soul to find rest in You.

Baptize me with the Holy Spirit! And maintain me as a vessel of righteousness worthy of Your grace.

Amen.

ON MEMORIAL DAY 2019

Dear God,

We are gathered here today to remember those who have made the ultimate sacrifice. As we gather, O Lord, we ask for Your tender mercies and unyielding grace upon those who have passed in the service of this great nation. We pray that Your angels may surround them and Your saints welcome them in peace. May they gaze upon You, face to face, and taste the blessedness of perfect rest.

It is through their grace that we find our grace.

It is through their courage that we find our courage.

It is through their faith in You, dear God, and their faith in this country that we come to understand that their sacrifices were not in vain.

Help us to remember them in our hearts.

Lord, we know that You are our hope and strength— and a very present help in trouble. So, as we honor Your humble servants today, may we always have hope and not fear. May we always remember to serve You as they have with a zeal for justice and the strength of forbearance. May we use the liberties that they have paid for in a just way in accordance with Your will.

Amen.

Prayer helps break the chains of societal bondage in an ego-driven world. It humbles us. In the midst of our struggles, we can come to the bended knee of our heart to acquiesce to One who is greater than ourselves—God.

PRAYERS FOR
GIVING
THANKS

THANK YOU, GOD

Dear God,

Thank you for the beauty of the day. In the midst of even the most tremendous storms You show us Your power and Your unyielding love.

Thank You for the majesty of even the smallest creatures You put in our midst. They show the magnitude of Your detail—and all its sophistication.

Thank You for how You have so wonderfully engineered us, sowing the seeds of love in us, so that even in our most brutal moments we can seek, find, and turn away from brutality.

Thank You for being a God who so willingly forgives our sins and allows us to come to grips with and let go of the vileness that can come upon us.

Finally, thank You for allowing us the privilege of drawing near You, so that in doing so we may evolve from being creatures lost in flesh to those found in Spirit. Thank You.

Amen.

A PRAYER OF THANKS
TO A NOURISHING GOD

Most Merciful and Gracious God,

We come to you on the bended knee of our hearts
to give thanks for Your provision of the bountiful fruits
in which we are about to partake for the nourishment
of our bodies. We know they are the fruits of those
who have labored from the fields to the kitchen, and
we thank You for the products of their work and ask
that You continue to bless them in their ministry of
providing sustenance.

We thank You for those whose loving hands have
prepared this meal. We know that they have seasoned
our food, not only with the spices that delight our
senses, but with the spirit that nourishes our souls. So,
when we are full, let us be full in our souls as well as
our bodies.

We are thankful that You have blessed us with
family and friends, that we may share the fruits of Your
bountiful harvest in community. We know that it is in
the gathering together and sharing as community that
we draw closer to You.

And God, we thank You for providing us a
community of souls from all corners of this earth and
walks of life, the blessings of the wealth of life, and the

love of each other. For we know that it is from the love You have imparted in us that all nourishment flows.

Amen.

When life is going just as we planned, or when it takes a sudden turn to sorrow or hardship or tragedy—God walks with us.

PRAYERS FOR
PEERLESS
VALUES

WHAT IS ETHICAL?

The messenger who had gone to summon Micaiah said to him, "Look, the words of the prophets with one accord are favorable to the king; let your word be like the word of one of them, and speak favorably." But Micaiah said "as the Lord lives, whatever the Lord says to me, that I will speak."
—I Kings 22:13–14 (NRSV)

What is popular is not always ethical.
What is ethical is not always popular.
The prudent person follows the ethical path,
because even when it is covered with thorns,
it is along that thorny path that we encounter wisdom.

TODAY'S PRAYER

Lord, help me to be humble,
that I may allow myself to
yield to Your will.

Help me to be compassionate,
that I may be kind to all I encounter,
regardless of station.

Help me to be strong,
and not lead into the temptation of hubris.

Help me to be merciful,
and not indulge in violence or deceit.

Help me to be loving, even to my enemies.
For love never fails.

Finally, help me to be thankful
for all the blessings of this life and the next
that You most surely have provided.

Amen.

A PRAYER TO BE FIRM

God,

Help me to stand in the midst of all that the world may give me. Keep me strong. I do not need the strength of body but the strength of spirit to always see Your works in my life. Guide me in times of trouble so that I may resist temptation. Help me to stand like a tree in a strong breeze, willing to bend but never break during the storm of sin that surrounds me. Let me always fear You who can take body and soul but not those who can take only my body. Keep me on the path of righteousness and let kindness and compassion guide me when I am dealing with others. And from morning to night, set Your Holy Spirit upon me so I may never forget that You sent Christ for the forgiveness of sins— so that I will always confess that He is my Lord and Savior. To You, dear God, be all honor, glory, and praise.

Amen.

A PRAYER FOR RESPECT

God,

You are no respecter of persons. You are just to the fatherless, the widowed, the exiled, those of high station, and those who are counted as the lowest in society. You see us all and You love us all. It is You whom I wish to serve and obey. You are the very definition of Love, and it is through You that I want to learn to respect all whom I encounter.

Help me to continually respect the significant person whom I love in my life so that our relationship is not built on physical attributes or based on needs of the flesh; rather, it is a connection of two souls living in harmony and longing for You, O God.

Help me to respect my children so that they may be raised to respect others and continually seek You, that they may come to understand what it is to dwell in a house where You are always present.

Help me to respect the sanctity of life to the point where I can live at peace with others regardless of who and what they are.

Help me to respect myself so that I can love myself and become an open vessel receptive to Your love and a willing disciple of Your Word.

Amen.

A PRAYER FOR INTEGRITY

God,

Help me to walk with an honest and true heart that seeks you. Draw me close to you each day of my life, that I may walk in the light of Your Truth. I do not want to be one of idle talk, always speaking Your name but allowing my heart to think and be a part of evil. I desire to earnestly love and praise You with all that I have in me.

Let my prayers not be spoken for the pleasure of the crowd but drawn from the depths of my soul to praise You. I would rather be silent and let You know that I love and seek You—not loud and arrogant, speaking Your name with a heart of stone. I would rather walk alone in a life of integrity than stand with a crowd of those who flirt with evil.

I will refuse to take part in anything that will separate me from You, O God. Do not allow me to sink to the level of those who spread lies and deceit that threaten to poison your world. Let my eyes and my heart continually gaze upon the heavens, that I will always seek to do righteousness in my life. Grant me the peace and justice that can only be found with a life truly lived with You.

Amen.

A PRAYER FOR HUMILITY
THROUGH SILENCE

God,
A flood of words is never
without its faults!
Please let the words of my mouth
and the meditation of my heart
always be acceptable to You.
I no longer wish to defile myself or others
by spouting venom that strangles the heart.
I want to be silent and know that You are God.
In that silence, I pray the Holy Spirit gives me my
voice.
Let a meditative spirit be my roadmap
to that place of peace Your Son has prepared for me.
Empty me of words but fill me with the Word;
So that in the quietness of my soul,
I may always seek, revere, and praise You.
Amen.

A PRAYER FOR EQUALITY

You shall remember that you were a slave in the land of Egypt, and the Lord your God redeemed you.
—Deuteronomy 15:15 (NKJV)

God,

Help me to love my neighbor as I love myself. In a time when the anger, bigotry, and fear fueled by the Evil One attempt to become the standards of our behavior—make me an agent of love, compassion, and fairness.

Continue to instill in me the understanding that in our differences lay our strengths. Do not allow me to be fueled by the fear of those who are not like me, but create in me a spirit of Truth that shows me the greatness of life in every soul whom I meet. Let me never forget that You are the Author and Creator of life and that every life I encounter is sacred and worthy of respect because they are Your creation. Forgive me should I fall short of Your glory and continue to draw me close to You. Teach me forgiveness instead of anger, love instead of intolerance, and understanding instead of ignorance. Let me never grieve the Holy Spirit. And keep the name of your Son, Jesus Christ, continually on my lips and in my heart.

Amen.

A PRAYER OF RIGHTEOUSNESS

God,

Help us to live lives that are based not on our desires but what You desire in us. Fill our hearts with love. Let us be guided in the hope of the coming Christ. Through Him let us seek to transform the world. Help us to be instruments of peace and worthy receivers of Your continuing grace, O God. Make us patient in the dealings with others and compassionate in our desire to do good. Keep us humble in spirit and allow the Holy Spirit to dwell among us. Deliver us from the evil of the world that seeks to separate us from You and keep us forever drawn to the knowledge of the otherworldly promise You made through Your Son. Take from us the fears of the world that cause us to sin and instill in us the fear of You that gives us wisdom. And let that wisdom keep us constantly on the path of righteousness.

Amen.

Two of the most dangerous combinations in the world are ego masquerading as faith and arrogance masquerading as leadership. Two of the greatest combinations in the world are kindness with no conditions and wisdom based in humility.

PRAYERS FOR
AN ENLIGHTENED
COMMUNITY,
NATION, &
WORLD

COME, LET US REASON
TOGETHER—JANUARY 6, 2021

Come, now let us reason together, says the Lord.
—Isaiah 1:18 (RSV)

Dear Lord,

The very soul of our nation is at stake. We are torn by anger, frustration, and mistrust. Please do not forsake us. Bestow upon our leadership the wisdom to guide us in an equitable and compassionate manner, that we may engage one another with a humble spirit powered by mutual respect, despite the diversity of ideologies.

Lord, help us to have patience and understanding with each other. Keep us from breaking the boundaries of trust that serve to unite us. Deliver us from the temptation of violence. Where there is the threat of violence, lead us to peace. And preserve in us a peace that surpasses all understanding. Where there is hatred, engage us in sowing the seeds of love.

Lord, where do we put our hope? Our hope is in You. Keep us in a hope that transcends the wounds that seek to divide us. Instill in us a unity of purpose and spirit. Heal our nation.

Lord, we want to build a beloved community and restore the soul of a nation built on freedom. In the midst of our struggles, guide us so that we may live by the precepts of equality, justice, and truth. Set upon us a prayerful spirit that we may always be mindful of meditating on Your Word. Guide us in all times, that we may know we are forever walking in Your sight.

For the honor of Your Holy Name, we say, Amen.

ON MEMORIAL DAY 2016

Almighty God, we thank You this day to remember those, who by their very sacrifice, have allowed us to live as free people. They, the men and women of our armed services, whose sacrifice in the face of grave dangers in a world that has from time to time been racked by turmoil and war, have been the ones who stood in the face of danger as shining examples of courage and grace.

Help us preserve their memories and precious sacrifices in our hearts and minds. Let us not fall away from the standards of honor and truth that they, throughout the history of this country, have stood for. Give us grace to continue to love each other and be preservers of compassion in a world that is wracked by continuing human suffering.

God, we must always remember that those whom we honor today stand as a shining example of what can be accomplished through hope, courage, and the desire to do Your will. We stand on the shoulders of their sacrifice. Our legacy of greatness as a nation is bound in the spirit of righteousness that they have passed down from generation to generation.

So, Almighty God, continue to guide us, and we humbly beseech Thee that we may always be mindful of Your favor and will. Continue to bless our land and save us from pride and arrogance as You help us to defend our liberties, call us to righteousness, and lead us to peace.

We ask that You continue to have mercy on this nation and its people, and that we may always be grateful for those in our nation whose lives are the very symbol of justice, forbearance, and love. Through Your Holy Name we pray,

Amen.

GOD IS TOO BIG

God is too big to belong to one faith. Or one group of people. It is the height of arrogance and the lack of faith in God and, sadly, faith in human kind—to believe otherwise. We are all God's people, regardless of who we are.

Wherever we gather in praise of God is sacred, with no place more sacred than the other. Slavery, hatred, war, and all the most horrible abuses of humankind can be attributed to the "my sacred is better than yours" game.

Think about this: maybe God just wants us to respect and love each other.

LEADERS ARE ...

Leaders are compassionate.
Leaders are kind.

They base their actions in wisdom
and live by a code of ethics
built on integrity.
They possess a unique ability
to empower others.
They embody courage
and are strong in the face of adversity.
Yet they are gentle in the midst of loss.

Leaders inspire us to hope
when we are in the midst of struggle.

They define us by their character.
Their righteousness knows no bounds.
They are selfless and altruistic.
They touch us by their grace
and lift us by their virtue.

FOR DR. KING

20 January 2006

Dear God,

We are gathered here today to honor Dr. Martin Luther King Jr., a man whose prophetic voice called out this nation to a new covenant based on justice, peace, love and forgiveness. We ask, dear God, that we as a people may come to understand that there can only be real freedom in this world when we, as Your people, enter into a new covenant that will break the chains of our societal bondage.

We ask You to bring us from a society based on entitlement of a few to one where all may benefit in community.

- Free us from the sense of entitlement that spawns the twin siblings of hypocrisy and bigotry.
- Free us from the hatred and fear that lead to violence in our nation and the world.
- Free us from the bondage of old wrongs, that we may indulge in forgiveness.
- Free us from the hard-heartedness that continuously keeps us from giving to the poor in our communities.
- Free us from the necessity of war that kills not only our young men and women and those

whom we call our enemies but also sets a stain on the collective soul of this nation and the world.

- Bring us out of the wandering of our longing for the facades of our past and a created history, that we may come to know the truths of a history where You work among us.
- Grant us peace with understanding, love based in compassion, and justice based in forgiveness.
- Break the earthly bonds of our ignorance and give us the courage to love unselfishly, heal the wounds of a broken humanity, and bring the freedom of Your love from the greatest to the least—so that someday we as a nation and a world may join in communion to say these words of Dr King: "Free at last, free at last, Thank God Almighty, we are free at last."

Amen.

Let your heart speak to and listen for God. Everyday.

PRAYERS FOR
ETERNAL
LIFE

THANKS FOR THE EMPTY TOMB

God, thank You for the empty tomb!
In that empty tomb there is the fullness of life,
that gives us hope.
In that empty tomb there is the forgiveness of sins
that anchors our salvation.
In that empty tomb there is the resurrection of the
dead
that helps us to understand the promise of everlasting
life.
In that empty tomb there is a symbol
of Your unending love for a sinful world.
In that empty tomb there is the living Truth that
Christ lived, Christ died, and Christ will come again.

Amen.

KNOW GOD—KNOW LIFE

God,

I cannot live without You. I may have life in my body with my heart pumping and blood flowing through my veins. I may be able to speak, walk, and conduct myself as a human being with all the functions that allow me to survive in this world, but unless You are part of my life, then I truly am not amongst the living.

It is You who knew me in my mother's womb, and You who now sees in my heart at all times. It is You who gave His only begotten Son, that I may have the forgiveness of sins, and it is You who forgives me when I cannot forgive myself. It is You who will know me when I am departed from this life. And it is You who has through Jesus Christ blessed me with the promise of eternal life.

It is You who sends the Holy Spirit that I may be comforted. It is You who allows me to rest in the night and work in the day. It is You who allows me to be amongst believers, that I may dwell in the body of Your Son. It is in You that I may plant the seeds of hope that come from your Kingdom instead of the hopelessness that comes from the facade of materialism in the human kingdom.

In Your hallowed name is my salvation and

redemption, and I have but to utter Your praises from my lips. In You is the light for my soul when the darkness seeks to lead me to the depths of hell. You are my Alpha and Omega. My very existence in this life or any other is solely because of You!

I am but a dead limb on a dying tree when I do not have You in my life—because You *are* my life and the very meaning of life itself! Please do not depart from me! Please hear me as I cry out to You. Draw me to Your heart, that my heart may truly beat. And make my soul long for You so that at no moment do I ever forget ... that I cannot live without You.

Amen.

GOD'S GRACE IS SUFFICIENT
FOR ME

Do not weep for me
or mourn my passing.
I am living in God's heart.
For God's Grace is sufficient for me.

Do not look back and ask,
what could I have done,
or wonder if you did enough.
For your love was greater than all
the wealth of nations, and
your devotion was stronger than any physical bond
that can be comprehended.
Yet in all that strength,
God's Grace is sufficient for me.

Do not worry about the length of my life,
or if there was enough time to enjoy it.
I look upon it as a blessing.
It was a life well-lived in God's call.
Yes, this earthly body may have been riddled
with the pain a debilitating disease brings,
but my spirit was undaunted, and it soared
under the shadow of God's wings.
For God's Grace is sufficient for me.

You see, despite all that I went through in life,
all that I experienced—the pain, sorrow, laughter, joy,
    and fear—
I was comforted in my soul by a God who is good to
    us all and has brought me
near, to a house with many rooms.
For those of you who wondered if I suffered or I was
    in pain,
to you I say it could never be.
At my most painful times, when my body ached
and my mind questioned my fate,
I was fine and warmed by the thought that
God's Grace is sufficient for me.

So, do not look back on what was,
but look ahead at what can be.
Be hopeful, love each other, pray, and have faith,
for I have gone to God's heart.
There I can rest, for I know I am a humble servant
who has completed his journey.
I no longer suffer, and I'm not alone.
I have come full circle
from my mother's womb to my heavenly home.
I'll smile as I look upon you,
    for God's Grace is sufficient for me.

A PRAYER TO LIVE A
KINGDOM LIFE

God,
Please take me into your Kingdom.
I want to be Your humble servant.
Let me be wounded
in order to be made whole.
Let me bear the weight of the cross,
that I may come to understand
the heaviness of my sins.
Let me be crucified and persecuted,
and let me suffer the thorns of this life,
that I may never be comfortable
until I arrive at the next life with You.
Let me continually bless, anoint, and love others,
so that I may understand that Grace is not a gift
but an enduring task.
Let me be forsaken by humankind
but never forsaken by You.
Let me burn with desire
to have the praise of Your Son on my lips,
while the flame of the Holy Spirit
remains lit in me.
Finally, God, let me die to a life of sin,
that I may live a sanctified life with You.

Amen.

God knows. God Cares. God loves.
Christ walks among us.

ACKNOWLEDGMENTS

Josephine Johnson (Ma), my mother-in-law. She sat with me through some of my toughest moments. She prayed with me, studied the Bible with me, and listened to my prayers and sermons. She never lost faith in me. Love you, Ma! God bless you. May you rest in peace.

Reverend Edwin Muller, who brought me into prison ministry and guided me as a prison chaplain. Your theological approach to ministry has made an enduring impact on my calling as a chaplain. Thank you, Ed, for walking alongside me as I continue to learn to be a prison chaplain. Your presence in my life has been a blessing.

Bishop Joseph Ravenell and Sister Mary Ravenell, who mentored me as I trained for my calling as a pastor. You gave me a church home and showed me the infinite possibilities of ministry when your objective is the heart of God. Thank you for your grace, wisdom, and kindness.

I want to thank Colin Rolfe and Paul Cohen at Epigraph Publishing. This was the second time we have worked together, and I know I could not have done this without you. Dory Mayo, my editor, thank you for guiding me to a final product. Your wisdom and encouragement were an answer to my prayers when I was stuck and did not know which way to turn as we finished and published this book. You gave me direction.

ABOUT THE AUTHOR

Rev. Alfred R. Twyman Jr. believes in the power of prayer and it's ability to transform lives. He has worked in parish and prison ministry for more than twenty-four years as a pastor and chaplain, where he has lead prayer groups and taught prayer as a major pastoral technique to a variety of denominations. *As Long as I Have Breath* is a compilation of some of the prayers that Rev. Twyman has said over his years of ministry. He believes that prayer is a combination of hope, humility, and faith—and that it offers freedom and gives people a sense of place in the world. He insists that prayer provides a relationship with God that anchors and strengthens the soul.

Born and raised in Harpers Ferry, West Virginia, during the 1950s, Twyman grew up in a time of segregation when the Black Church and prayer meetings were essential to survival. He often says, "We lived to pray and prayed to live during those times."

Twyman is a retired Navy officer and graduate of the Naval War College, where he earned a master's degree in Strategic Theory and Foreign Affairs. He studied for pastoral ministry at Princeton Theological Seminary, where he earned a Master of Divinity (M.Div.) with a concentration in Christian Ethics. He was awarded the Princeton Seminary Ethics Award for his work in prison and urban ministry.

Rev. Twyman is an ordained minister in The Christian Church (Disciples of Christ) and holds standing in the United Church of Christ. He currently serves as a regional chaplain for the New York State Department of Corrections and Community Supervision.

www.ingramcontent.com/pod-product-compliance
Lightning Source LLC
LaVergne TN
LVHW011401080426
835511LV00005B/380